# A Note to Parents and Teachers

SAINSBURY'S READING SCHEME is a compelling new reading programme for children, designed in conjunction with leading literacy experts, including Cliff Moon M.Ed., Honorary Fellow of the University of Reading. Cliff Moon has spent many years as a teacher and teacher educator specializing in reading and has written more than 140 books for children and teachers. He reviews regularly for teachers' journals.

Beautiful illustrations and superb full-colour photographs combine with engaging, easy-to-read stories to offer a fresh approach to each subject. Each book in the SAINSBURY'S READING SCHEME programme is guaranteed to capture a child's interest while developing his or her reading skills, general knowledge and love of reading.

The five levels of the programme are aimed at different reading abilities, enabling you to choose the books that are exactly right for your child:

**Yellow Level** – Learning to read
**Green Level** – Beginning to read
**Gold Level** – Beginning to read alone
**Ruby Level** – Reading alone
**Sapphire Level** – Proficient readers

The "normal" age at which a child begins to read can be anywhere from three to eight years old, so these levels are only a general guideline.

No matter which level you select, you can be sure that you are helping your child learn to read, then read to learn!

LONDON, NEW YORK, MUNICH,
MELBOURNE AND DELHI

**Project Editor** Caryn Jenner
**Art Editor** Jane Horne
**Senior Art Editor** Clare Shedden
**Series Editor** Deborah Lock
**Production** Shivani Pandey
**Picture Researcher** Angela Anderson
**Jacket Designer** David McDonald

**Space Consultant**
Carole Stott

**Reading Consultant**
Cliff Moon M.Ed.

This edition published in 2011
First published in Great Britain in 2001 by
Dorling Kindersley Limited
80 Strand, London WC2 0RL
Penguin Group (UK)

Copyright © 2001 Dorling Kindersley Limited

2 4 6 8 10 9 7 5 3 1
001–MB142P–Jun/11

A CIP catalogue record for this book is
available from the British Library.

ISBN 978-1-4053-7560-3

Colour reproduction by Colourscan, Singapore
Printed and bound in China by L. Rex Printing Co. Ltd.

The publisher would like to thank the following for their
kind permission to reproduce their images:
Position key: c=centre; b=bottom; l=left; r=right; t=top

**European Space Agency**: 19t, 20t, 29c; N.A.S.A.
24-25 background. **Eurospace Centre, Transinne, Belgium**: 6-7,
stickers cla. **London Planetarium**: 6. **N.A.S.A.**: Front cover, 4, 5, 8,
9tr, 9b, 10-11, 12-13, 14, 15, 16-17, 18, 26tl, 28-29, 31, stickers tr, cr.
**Planet Earth Pictures**: 22-23, 22b. **Space and Rocket Center,
Alabama**: 24-25 foreground. **Science Photo Library**: 26-27.
**N.A.S.A. Kennedy Space Center**: front jacket, back jacket.
**Paul Weston**: illustration 30cl.

All other images © Dorling Kindersley.
For further information see: www.dkimages.com

Discover more at

# www.dk.com

Sainsbury's
Reading Scheme

Green Level
**Beginning to read**

# Rockets
## and Spaceships

Written by Karen Wallace

5... 4... 3... 2... 1...
Blast Off!

Rumble... rumble...
ROOAAARRRR!
A rocket takes off
into the sky.
It zooms up and
away from Earth.

rocket

The rocket flies very far,
VERY FAST.

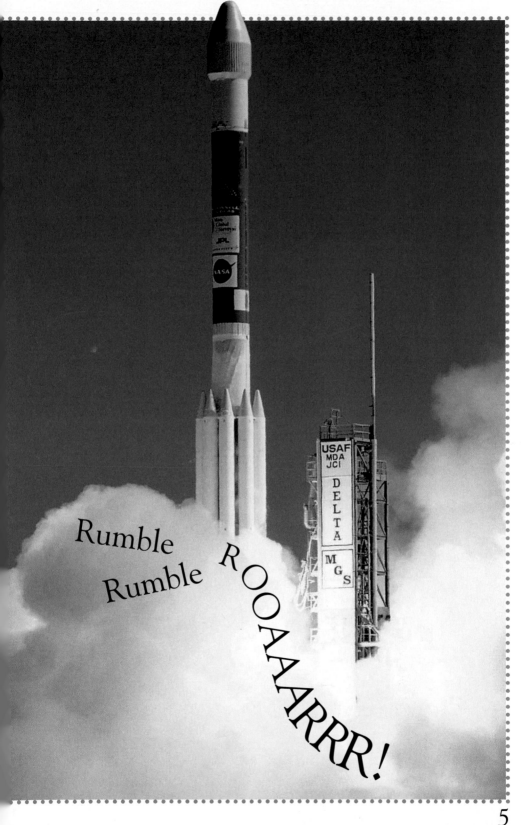

Rumble Rumble ROOAAARRR!

Rockets help us
to explore space.
Astronauts are scientists
who travel in space.

astronaut

They travel in a spaceship
at the top of a rocket.

The rocket takes
the spaceship up to space.
Then the rocket falls away.

Astronauts can see
the Moon and stars in space.
They can see planets, too.
Our planet is called Earth.
This is how astronauts see Earth
from space.

Some astronauts have travelled
to the Moon.
They explored the Moon
and did experiments.

They picked up
dust and rocks
for scientists to study
back on Earth.

Sometimes, astronauts "walk" in space. Walking in space is not like walking on Earth.

Astronauts must use a special rope,
which keeps them
attached to their spaceship.
Otherwise, they would float away!

This is a space shuttle.
It is part rocket, part plane.
Astronauts have used it
for many trips to space.
The plane part of the space shuttle
can be used again and again.
It takes off like a rocket,
then it glides back to Earth
and lands like an aeroplane.

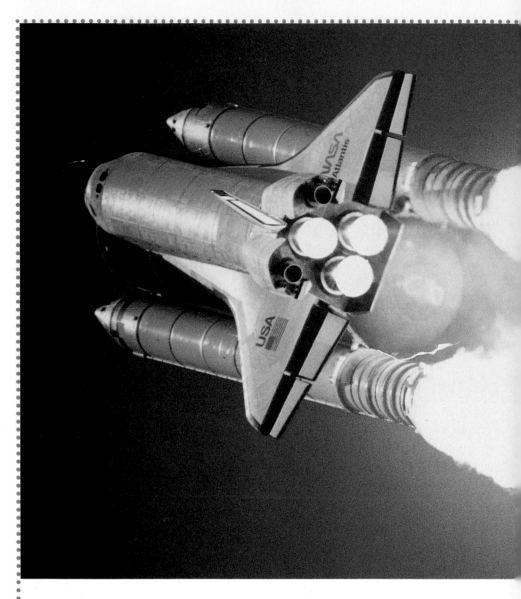

The space shuttle uses
rocket engines to blast off.
When the rocket engines fall away
the shuttle plane flies into space.

A space shuttle does
many different jobs.
It can carry satellites
as well as astronauts.

satellite

Different kinds of satellites
do different jobs from space.
Special computers
help the satellites keep
their correct position
above the Earth.

The satellites send
and receive signals,
which help us every day.

Some satellites send signals from one part of the world to another.

We use these signals when we watch television or talk on the telephone.

Other satellites
take pictures
of the weather from
high above Earth.

This picture shows
a storm coming!

The Hubble
Space Telescope
is a very
special satellite.

It is a telescope
and a camera,
which can see
stars and planets
that are millions of
kilometres (miles) away.

The planet
in this picture
is called Saturn.

Saturn

Probes are machines
that explore space
on their own.
They do not carry
astronauts.

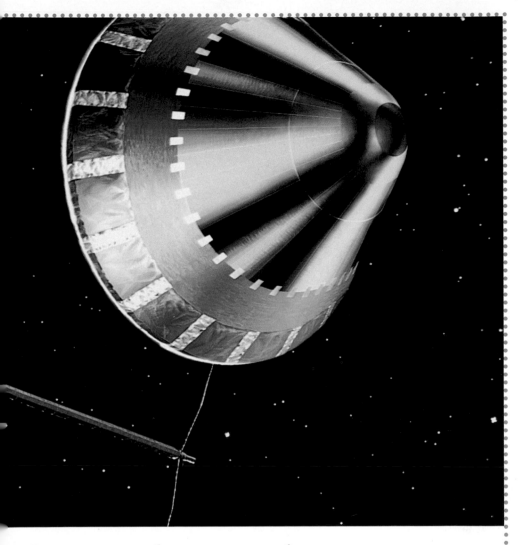

Space probes visit planets
that are very far away.
They take pictures and
send them back
to scientists on Earth.

Mars

A space probe carried
this tiny buggy
to a planet called Mars.
The buggy explored Mars and
studied the rocks.

Some people think
there might be
life on Mars.
One day, scientists
will know for sure!

Some astronauts
stay in space
for months
and months.

The space station
becomes their home.
They do experiments
and learn about
living in space.

Imagine eating
and sleeping
in a place
where everything floats!

There are still so many secrets
to discover.

Scientists invent new rockets
and spaceships all the time.
There are even plans
to build a space hotel.

Greetings from **space**

Who knows?
One day **you** might go
on holiday in space!

# Glossary

## Astronaut
a person trained to travel in a spaceship and to work in space.

## Mars
the fourth planet from the Sun looks a red colour.

## Rocket
a vehicle with a rocket engine that can travel through space.

## Satellite
a man-made space object that goes around Earth, sending back information.

## Saturn
the sixth planet from the Sun has seven thin rings of ice around it.